A Parents' Guide

to

College Soccer Recruiting

By John Steven

A Special Thanks

While I can't mention all of the coaches that have had an impact on the lives of our children, the most profound effect certainly came from their High School Coach and their Club's Director of Coaching. While you will remain nameless, I hope you understand how much you mean to our family.

I would like to dedicate this guide to my four beautiful daughters who have not only performed on the soccer field but in the classroom as well. I am so proud of all the things you have accomplished and am excited about all the great things you will become. Your Mom and I are so blessed. We Love You!

Also, many thanks to MaryPat Hosler for her creative work on the guide's cover!

Disclaimer

The opinions and views contained herein are those of the author. The reader accepts and understands that if any portion of this guide is used and applied at any learning institution with any representative of the learning institution for soccer recruiting, the reader assumes all outcomes and all risks in its application, including financial loss. The author presents this material without warranty or accuracy of any kind, expressed or implied, foreseen or unforeseen and will not be held liable for the unsuccessful use of the material.

Reproduction

ISBN: 1449971881
EAN-13: 9781449971885
Additional copies can be ordered via the internet

Contents

Introduction

Introduction

If you are reading this guide you have enjoyed many years of watching your son or daughter compete at a high soccer skill level and have made incredible friends along the way. All of us have a complete love for the game of soccer and for our children. Ensuring that they are comfortable with their four year university commitment is important to every parent. You will need to help guide your son or daughter through the endless amount of information that will bombard them over a short period of time. I will tell you right off the bat, it won't be easy! This guide is intended to provide you with some insight into the recruiting process. I have found that very few parents understand the process and simply go along for the recruiting ride, sometimes literally.

I have one son and four daughters. While my son played high school soccer, my daughters played high school soccer, club, Olympic Development Program (ODP) and are all now playing or finishing playing Division 1 soccer. Through the hundreds of hours between all four of their recruiting processes, I have learned a lot. I wrote this guide to share some of my experiences with those of you going through this for the first time so you can benefit from my trials and experiences.

I still remember my oldest daughter's process. I had no idea what the coach expected, what he would say or what I needed to consider. I must admit, I felt like an idiot the first time around! I am hoping this guide will make it easier for you. Recruiting can be a very stressful and confusing process to you and your young adult, however you may be fortunate enough to have a university help with the enormous financial burden of the university experience.

Hindsight is 20/20

One of the biggest lessons I learned is to start planning in advance. Several years *prior* to beginning the recruiting process,

A Parents' Guide To College Soccer Recruiting

I would focus energy on any academic *and* soccer weaknesses. Academic weaknesses would be indicated in Math and English standardized exams as well as grades. I would have also request feedback from several coaches on soccer strengths and weaknesses. This would ensure there would be no obstacles in the way of your son or daughter's final choice. This is covered in detail in Chapter 4, The Coaches Perspective.

Understanding Your Son or Daughter's Goals as a Player

What commitment to soccer does your son or daughter want to make at the college level? I think this is an important question for them to consider before they think about playing in college. To play Division 1 soccer, they must be ready to give up some social and weekend activities. Division 1 practices are usually four days a week and two to four hours a day. They are scheduled at specific times during the week, and can be as early as 6AM or, in the case of one of my daughters, running a fitness test in August at midnight. Conditioning work such as lifting weights and running is continuous. Weekends are usually filled with games and travel. Since soccer is played during the fall semester, the spring semester is filled with training and conditioning to increase strength and speed. During the summer months, coaches expect that their team members will continue to play to stay sharp. Coaches frown upon athletes that get significant scholarships having full time summer jobs. Some coaches believe that they are already getting paid in terms of a scholarship and should focus their time on improving their skills and being ready for the kick off of the summer practices. In addition, coaches expect that athletes come back from the summer in shape able to pass fitness tests to continue to play. A Division 1 coach stated "If you don't love soccer enough to live it, breathe it throughout the year, and are willing to make it a priority, you shouldn't play Division 1 soccer". Athletes that are not willing to make this commitment will not last long on a

A Parents' Guide To College Soccer Recruiting

Division 1 soccer program. Keep in mind athletes who don't want to make the commitment to Division 1 soccer can continue to play in college leagues. Most schools have intramurals / club soccer that will allow them to play without the commitment mentioned above.

The Craziness of the Recruiting Cycle

As of the writing of this guide, university coaches are beginning their recruiting process earlier and earlier. High school sophomores and sometimes freshmen are being scouted and in some cases being asked to make a "verbal commitment" to a college that is three or four years away. Division 1 university coaches are taking regional and national soccer coaching jobs to enable them to scout the best talent, develop relationships with the players and promote their institutions. Other coaches are promoting soccer camps to allow more opportunities to scout possible athletes and ok.. make some additional money. Recruiting is being conducted at a point when young kids are not ready or able to make a commitment or decision. Unless the NCAA does something about the recruiting cycle, I expect that kids will continue to get recruited earlier and earlier.

Financial Drain on Parents

Nothing, I repeat nothing is covered by the university for recruiting expenses until the first day of class of your son or daughter's senior year in high school. Visits prior to this date will come out of the "money tree" which means you! These visits are referred to by the university as "Unofficial Visits." This simply means that you will pay for everything on your recruiting trip, from transportation to lodging and meals. Normally, if your son or daughter is spending the night during their college visit, the university will ask for a lodging payment. This is normally a pretty small amount; maybe $20 or $30 dollars. The really unfortunate side to the current recruiting process is that only families that can afford air travel and all the expenses that go along with it can look at colleges outside of their immediate geographic location.

Once the recruiting cycle begins, you need to put in a lot of time, effort and money for your son or daughter in a relatively short period of time. As such, start saving money several months ahead of time. Hopefully this will make the burden easier. Normally, by the time your son or daughter has made a decision, coaches will invite their recruits to the university for an "Official Visit" where all expenses are paid. Again, this will only be possible after the recruits first day of class in their senior year of high school, and in many cases, recruiting at Division 1 schools has finished. Funny how things work out, huh!

Division 1, 2 and 3 Designations

This was confusing to me when I first started helping the kids with all of the communications from the universities. What can a Division 1 school provide that a Division 2 or Division 3 school can't?
Division 1 schools are able to provide fully or partially funded athletic scholarships. If they are *partially* funded, they may only have 8 full scholarships. In these situations the coaches may give one or two full scholarships and the remaining players will be offered a fraction based on the value they think the player brings to the team. So, Sarah gets 60% and Mary gets 40%.

A fully funded Division school means that they can have up to 14 full scholarships for women's soccer and 9.9 for men. This is the maximum allowed by the NCAA as of the writing of this guide. Needless to say, these programs can offer you a better economic value as there is more money to spread around. However, be careful to find out how many athletes the coach has on the roster. The NCAA views soccer as an "equivalency sport" which means coaches can divide the money among a large number of players. I have heard of some coaches carrying 25 to 30 soccer players thus thinning the scholarship opportunities out even more. In addition, some partially funded programs will try to add other funding sources such as academic or financial need based scholarships or grants.

A designation as a Division 1 school has no correlation to the school's size but has everything to do with the sports they designate as being funded for scholarships and Division 1 level. Some universities have designated one sport as a Division 1 program and the rest of the sports in their program may be Division 2 or 3. A Division 1 school must field men and women athletes in at least 7 sports or 14 total teams. Also, a Division 1 school may not be as good academically as a Division 3 school and a Division 3 school and be bigger than a Division 1 school.

Division 2 universities are usually partially funded through athletic aid. They tend to have small amounts of money to offer and will try to find creative ways to help with the cost of an education. This tends to be in academic or financial need based grants. They become very creative in their funding sources. They must sponsor at least 5 women's and men's sports with a commitment to participate in a certain number of contests.

Division 3 schools do not offer athletic scholarships. They rely on academic scholarships and student owned loans. They must sponsor at least 5 women and 5 men sports. It should be noted that Ivy League schools do not provide athletic scholarships but can reduce the GPA requirement for an athlete to get accepted.

Coach's Dilemma

In many situations, when coaches are recruiting they are looking for replacements for their graduating players or to fix a problem they had in the previous year's team. They have a relatively short window of time to assess an athlete's skill level and begin the recruiting process. They pay attention to the level of soccer that your son or daughter has attained and look for specific physical attributes /characteristics. I over heard two coaches talking about the problems with recruiting young girls so early. One coach explained to the other that she had recruited a sophomore in high school who had wonderful technical skills and speed but by the time she graduated high school she had gained 20 pounds and moved slower than molasses uphill in the middle of a snow storm. It seems that everyone is complaining about how early kids are being recruited but little is being done to resolve the problem.

High School/Club versus College Level Soccer

As one standout high school and club player stated "College level soccer is faster and more physical than high school and club soccer. Most athletes on each team are the best of the best from their respective high school and club teams." Another player stated "Not like high school where you can simply run around players and score.. each play is a fight and only determination will win." Referees will not call the same fouls in college, and expect players to be able to handle the physical punishment. Level set your son or daughter and make them realize that most everyone in fast, physical and strong. Hitting the college ranks brings new challenges as they compete against the very best.

Chapter 1

Positioning a Player to be Recruited

Exposure, exposure, exposure. Recruiting is in many respects like marketing. Making sure your son or daughter is seen often and by the right schools is key. Admittedly, it can be a determining event that will provide or kill an opportunity with a school based on a poor showing. But in general, the more exposure the more opportunities.

Tournaments

There are many "Coaches Tournaments" scheduled throughout the year. As of the writing of this guide, getting into elite tournaments during your son or daughter's sophomore and junior high school year is critical. Unfortunately, getting into these tournaments depends on your club team's record within the league and the tournaments won. Coaches really like these tournaments since they are able to see many athletes in a short period of time. If your team does not get in an elite tournament, many tournaments allow "Guest Players" to be added to teams through the tournament's web site or by contacting the teams directly. In general, they will normally guarantee you a certain amount of playing time, but chances are your son or daughter will not start a game.

The Correct Tournaments

There are local, regional and national Coaches' tournaments that are held during most every holiday and weekends that local clubs are not playing. Having your club pick the right coaches' tournaments based on an understanding of where each player would like to go to school and the downstream expenses should be considered. In all of my years working through the recruiting process and asking hundreds of parents where their son or daughter are going to go to school, not one player, whether a national, regional or club player, ever said they are going to play on the west coast or for that matter west of Ohio. Going west may have been an option but never was the final decision. I am sure, in most cases, parents on the west coast rarely send their sons or daughters to the east or if in the plain states to the east or west. What that tells me is that in most cases, distance plays a huge factor in the decision process so picking the correct "regional" tournaments is the key. So the question is why play in Coaches' tournaments that are more than 600 miles away from home? I use the number 600 as this seems to be the longest I can stay in a car in one day! Airfare, hotel, car rental, food etc, etc.. all add up during the recruiting process and certainly become a hindrance should a school be selected more than 600 miles away. It seems to me that in the end most athletes stay local. There are exceptions to this general observation such as your club team wishes to establish a high national ranking that would attract more coaches to "regional" Coaches' tournaments. It also occurs for parent reasons (I went there... you're going there). If your son or daughter is determined to "get away" and your happy about that concept, many large universities send their coaches to the larger "regional" tournaments... therefore traveling more than 600 miles is still not necessary and becomes the expense of the visiting university! I think this is a valued conversation your team and coach should have before the recruiting process begins.

Tournament Communication with Coach

It is important to know that coaches who are coming to these tournaments are not allowed to communicate with you, the parent, or your son or daughter during the tournament. According to NCAA rules they are allowed to say hello but must take the appropriate action to stop the conversation. Not knowing this makes for an embarrassing situation. I saw one of the coaches that scheduled one of my daughters earlier in the month for a visit. Feeling like I got to know them a bit better, I walked up to him and said hello. He responded and said hello. He then turned the other way and started watching the game without any further eye contact or explanation. Needless to say I was a bit ticked off with him and thinking something had gone wrong in the recruiting process with that school. Later, I spoke with one of our club coaches about the incident and he explained the rule. I still forget the rule from time to time but now understand the cold shoulder.

Olympic Development Program (ODP)

Having your son or daughter try-out and make the ODP program in your state is another way to expose them to additional college coaches. Each year, kids in specific age groups try-out for the state team. I have heard some college coaches say that they require ODP when considering the player. Coaches who coach these teams tend to be higher level coaches from local universities or have earned higher certificates in the art of coaching. Each year there are regional ODP tournaments going on within the United States. Depending on the age group, the winners of the regional tournaments may then compete at the national level where the winner of each regional tournament will play each other. College coaches visit these regional tournaments for recruiting purposes. ODP is not cheap and is an additional financial burden that may be a good investment in the long run. The way I positioned ODP with our kids was to suggest that if they plan to play Division 1 soccer they should get into the ODP program. One suggestion with ODP, your son or daughter should start as early as possible as relationships are built over the years among the players and coaches. These relationships may be hard to build if you start too late.

Club Coach's Relationships with the Universities

If your son or daughter has a specific university in mind, talk with your club coach to see if they know the coach of that university. Many of the coaches know each other from coaching conferences, working as an ODP coach or in other social ways. If they have a good relationship with that university, their feedback is taken seriously by the university coaches and is a great way to be seen. Understand however, that no straight shooting coach is going to recommend a player who is not at that universities level of soccer. Their reputation will be tarnished and they will loose the respect of that coach and likely other coaches as well. The other possibility is to have your coach make contact with the university during the tournaments or by phone or email prior to the tournament. It is therefore important that prior to a Coaches' tournament, your son or daughter discusses with your club coach what schools they are interested in so the coach can make contact with these schools and encourage them to review your son or daughters play. This may be the extra push, over and above the emails and phone calls that you have already made to get the coach to stop by and see your son or daughter.

University Summer Soccer Camps

Summer soccer camps are another way for college coaches to look closer at a potential recruit. As long as the university that is putting on the camp is not out of your son or daughters league of play, this may be another good method to be seen. Many times a university that has recruited an athlete will ask them to come to the camp prior to starting their freshman year. Getting an invite to a summer soccer camp is nothing special in most cases. It does provide another set of eyes to advice on improvements and additional revenue to the coaches and university depending on the arrangements.

Club Loyalty Versus Selling Your Son or Daughter Short

To be seen in the right tournaments and by the most coaches as possible, you must have a team that can compete at the highest level. Most leagues call the top performing soccer group "Premier" but what ever your club and league call it, you must be in the top level group. Unless you are two to three years out from the recruiting process and have time to get back into the top performing league, I would seriously look at moving to a team that is performing at a higher level. While I feel I am a very loyal person, I had to do it with one of my daughters. In the end, it was the best decision for her future. This decision should be made with your coach, your daughter or son and with you, the parent. In most cases this decision will be extremely difficult because of the relationships your son and daughter and you have with the team. One word of caution however, jumping from one club to another can become an issue to coaches, players and parents whether you are on the receiving or departing side. Both teams will begin to question you the parent and your son or daughters commitment to any team.

Be Honest About Your Son or Daughters Capabilities

When you begin the recruiting process, be honest about which universities you should focus your attention. I have seen so many parents wanting their kids to contact and be recruited by universities that are simply out of their caliber of play. Ask your coaches where they think your son or daughter would be best situated among the different division schools. If your son or daughter has a specific school in mind, ask the coach if they believe it's attainable. From this discussion you will be much better off than wasting your time and money visiting a university that has no interest as they have the best players to choose from. The other point, and possibly more important, is if your son or daughter gets recruited at a top-rated soccer school, will your son or daughter ever play? Will they simply be an orange soccer cone on a field that will be used by the other athletes for practice? I know of several girls who were very good players but have received very little if any playing time. That would not be fun.

Chapter 2

The Recruiting Cycle

Knowing how the recruiting cycle works is very important in positioning your son or daughter with the best schools and the best scholarship offer. Many people I've talked to believe the recruiting cycle is based on their own personal schedule or they leave it totally up to their son or daughter to start the process… and you know how that goes…nothing happens most of the time! There is an approximate start and end date to the cycle and it varies by university but you need to know both.

Know When the Recruiting Cycle Starts

The first thing to know about the recruiting cycle is to know when it starts. In general, the large Division 1 schools that have a history of great programs begin the recruiting process earlier than other schools. Some of them are finishing up their recruiting process when other Division 1 schools are just beginning. Finding out when they are recruiting players is a great way to know when you have to begin your process. The first place to discuss the recruiting cycle is with you club or ODP coach. Be sure the coach really knows when the cycle starts and don't accept an answer of "don't worry.. you have plenty of time." Ask universities that your son or daughter may be interested in pursuing when they will begin their recruiting process. This may be in the spring or summer of your son or daughters sophomore year, possibly earlier depending on the school.   If you know a national or regional player check with them from time to time to see who has begun their recruiting process. This will put you in a better position for your own recruiting cycle. Some of my daughters lost possible opportunities with some well known schools because we started our inquiries to late. Don't let this happen to you!

Start the Recruiting Process at the Right Time

Don't start the recruiting process to early. Going to a school early does not put your son or daughter in a situation of choice.

A Parents' Guide to College Soccer Recruiting

20

Many colleges will try to pressure your son or daughter to make a decision before other schools have had the opportunity to watch them play. It also makes it difficult to remember later in the process what your son or daughter liked about the school. <u>When you start the selection process, there should be a steady stream of visits.</u>

Committing Too Early

Don't commit too early in the process. Unless you receive an offer from the school that your son or daughter has always dreamed about, give the process some more time. In general, coaches will allow you time to make visits to other schools without too much pressure. They will let you know when they need a decision. In some situations, they will tell your son and daughter that they have a specific amount of weeks or days to make up their mind before going to the next recruit.

Committing Too Late

Don't commit too late in the process either. Stringing out a decision is not something a coach will appreciate, and in some cases can have devastating results. Coaches will hang in there for awhile however, if they are not getting positive feedback or your son or daughter is unresponsive, they will move on. You want to avoid getting the following message: "Despite several emails/letters to your [son] or [daughter] we have not received a response that indicated they are interested in our program and therefore we have moved on with our recruiting search". A steady communication stream with the coach will ensure they know your son or daughter's interest level.

The Ebb and Flow of the Recruiting Cycle

The recruiting cycle starts ends and restarts several times. There are a lot of things going on behind the scenes that neither you, the parent, nor your son or daughter will see. Coaches may put one recruit off a bit because another player is showing interest. They have already told one player they are interested but this other athlete shows more promise, so they offer the first kid the "right to play" but give them nothing monetarily. Always remember this is a business to the universities and the coach. Coaches may have you come to the university for several visits and in the end offer nothing as their recruiting process is always changing and evolving. You need to understand and be aware of what's going on behind the scenes and ensure you have options no matter how much they say they love your son or daughter.

Recruiting Techniques by Coaches

Universities have several techniques used in the recruiting process. In some cases a broad recruiting net is cast to hundreds of athletes to determine who is interested and provide more choices. Players respond and a recruiting ladder is built. Plans are developed to see as many girls/guys as possible during coaches' tournaments where each player is evaluated further. Some players are dropped, meaning there is no further communication with the player, or further communication is initiated by the coach to keep the athlete's interest alive while looking at other potential athletes. This can really be confusing to your son or daughter who may be interested in the university but getting little to no communication or simply told "No we're not interested" without an explanation. Coaches also put their recruiting pool on mailing lists to provide articles on the team and selected players. I would not place much confidence in receiving these mailings. In one case, one of my daughters had to ask the coach to please stop sending her information unless they were truly interested.. which they weren't.. but the mail kept coming!

The Pecking Order for Players

There seems to be a pecking order in the recruiting process that is understood and accepted by most coaches. Most national and regional players will be the first to be recruited at the premier schools. Some of these players will commit to premier schools very early in the recruiting process. When players commit to one school, it may open a slot on another teams recruiting ladder where a coach was competing for the same player. Once the recruiting needs are met at the premier schools, available players then drop to other Division 1 schools until their recruiting needs are met. The player pool then drops to small Division 1 schools where the cycle is again completed until Division 2/3 schools select the other good players that are available.

Of course, there are exceptions such as Division 3 schools where academic reputation is of more value than competition and athletic scholarships. Players may also receive an academic scholarship and will have the choice to go to any school. Players may simply like a particular university over another and playing for a big name school is not important.

Being in the upper recruiting class has everything to do with the players credentials. In general, national and regional players are first tier, ODP and club player's are second tier and club and sometime high school experience are the final tier of player selection. While this is arguable, this is what I have observed.

Managing the Recruiting Process Around Injuries

As we all know, soccer is a physical sport and as such players get hurt. Injuries such as bruises, broken bones, concussions or the dreaded ACL knee injury happen all too often. So when an injury hits your son or daughter in the recruiting cycle, what should you do? The answer is not easy and depends on when the injury occurs. If the injury is something minor such as a pulled muscle or sprained ankle that does not stop your son or daughter from playing, but will have a performance hit, simply let the recruiting coaches know about the injury prior to a tournament. Failing to let the coach know could have negative consequences in the recruiting process for obvious reasons. On the other hand, don't report every small problem either, coaches love tough kids!

If you have a major injury, such as a broken bone or an ACL injury, careful communication is needed to keep coaches interested. If the injury occurs at the beginning of the recruiting cycle, you should still communicate with each of the coaches as you would if your son or daughter were not hurt. Emphasize in your emails the past accomplishments and levels of soccer attained. Also important is to let the coach know that you are recovering from an injury and when you expect to play again. An athlete should never play in a coaches' tournament or any soccer activities for that matter, until cleared by a doctor to play. I have seen athletes start playing prior to their bodies healing with devastating results.

If your major injury occurs near the end of the recruiting process, you need to determine if the schools who have recruited your son or daughter are your top choices and then keep the communication lines open. If not, continued work to line up other schools once your son or daughter is healed should be the task at hand. Will your son or daughter miss out on some opportunities as a result of a major injury? Absolutely. Will coaches become disinterested in your son or daughter as a player should a major injury? Yes, some do, but having a major injury does not prevent you from finding other good schools. One of my daughters suffered an ACL injury in May of her sophomore year in high school. As a result, she missed several major ODP and Coaches' Tournaments and missed the recruiting cycle for several large programs. She came back to play in March of her junior year and played in several Coaches' tournaments. While I must admit, there were fewer opportunities available, it became very evident that there were some. What I failed to consider was all of the open slots on teams not generated by seniors, but by students who simply quit, coaches that terminated scholarships for one reason or another, players who transferred to another universities' soccer team or had to leave because of academic performance. This does not include the schools that would provide a scholarship the second, third and forth year but not the first due to depleted funds. Once your son or daughter is back and ready to go, your club coach should become your advocate to solicit interest from college coaches. So if this should happen to your son or daughter.. keep your chin up!

Chapter 3

Considerations Before the Recruiting Dance

There are several things to think about before starting the recruiting dance. Things like area of study, finances, school location and size, grades and travel are just a few of the many considerations to think about before the process begins.

Academic Fit

If your son or daughter knows the area of study they are interested in pursuing, this will add another variable in the recruiting process. Different schools have different areas of expertise. These areas may be business, law, premed, physical therapy, engineering and so on. If your son or daughter is interested in a specific area of study, you will need to start your recruiting process by researching which universities have schools in your son or daughter's area of interest. Next, communicating this proactively with the coach will have immense value.

Another consideration is selecting a school that will challenge your son or daughter in the classroom. On the other hand, if your son or daughter is not strong in the classroom, selecting an academically challenging school may only frustrate them. Finding the right academic level for you son or daughter is important in the recruiting process. University rankings and information of the schools within the university can also be found on the internet.

Picking the Right School

If your son or daughter has several offers and everything is equal, meaning scholarships are generally the same and the coach and university each have their pros and cons it can be challenging to pick the right school. Let me explain. One of my daughters was in a situation where she had several options on the table. One of the options was a poor academically ranked university that had a very nice coach. She wanted to go to that school because some of her old teammates were going there. When this university was brought up as one of the options to a competing coach, the response was "Why would she want to go to a university that is not academically ranked?" I told him the truth which was "she has selected this school based on friendships and not necessarily what's best for her." After dealing with the emotional side of this process, I now realize how ridiculous this sounded when I saw the look on the coach's face. This quickly pointed out to me that decisions my kids make at this age are sometimes based on emotions and friendships rather than experience and data. When an employer looks at his/her resume in the future, which school is more likely to impress? Pick the right school even if it means having to shell out some money.

Getting Key Information to Contact a Coach/University

To initiate discussions with a university, I have found the following technique quite effective. Using the internet, find the women's or men's athletic web page and complete the on-line recruiting questionnaire. By doing a little poking around, you should be able to find the staff directory which usually lists the head coach and assistant coach email addresses. Help your son or daughter write a formal email expressing interest in the school and the soccer program. This is covered in more detail later in this guide. Coaches are interested in hearing from players who they know are interested in their program and not just a scholarship.

Can you Afford the School You're Courting?

It is very important to know how expensive a school is before the recruiting process begins. This is especially important if you are paying! Schools can range from $12,000 to $60,000 or more a year depending on in-state or out-of-state designation. You can find this information by searching on the universities web page for "tuition board and fees". If a large university is recruiting your son or daughter and the yearly tuition, board and fees are $30,000 and they provide a 50% scholarship are you willing and able to pay $15,000 per year? $15,000 maybe more than most state schools.

Paying for Your Decision

Unless you have unlimited funds, identify how you will pay for the part of the bill that is not covered by the scholarship. Will it be home equity, student loan, prepaid college program or other grants or combination of the above? Having a financial plan that is effective for you or your son or daughter to repay is a good tactic in the upcoming negotiation process. I personally don't like home equity loans as a source of funding as it uses your house for collateral. If for some reason you lose your job because of a down turn in the economy or other such event your home becomes at risk. If you go that route for tax purposes, be sure you have the cash to back the loan. Using student loans, even if you plan to pay for the education may provide an additional four years of saving time as they don't become due until your son or daughter graduates. FAFSA (Free Application for Federal Student Aid) is a loan that can also be a possibility to help fund their college expense. Having a high family income will not disqualify you for this loan necessarily. Funds are limited and is first come first serve so you must apply on January 1st of you son or daughters senior year of high school. Go to www.fafsa.gov for more information.

Setting and Size

It helps to know if your son or daughter is interested in a city school, campus setting, big school or small school, a ranked university or well know university. Getting an understanding of the environment in which you son or daughter wants to spend his/her four years is also important in the recruiting process. They may want a university with a football team, hockey team, rowing or whatever they enjoy watching or doing in their spare time. In the end, there are trade-offs that your son or daughter will make in the selection process and what *you* think they might like may look nothing like their final decision.

Grades and Test Scores – Sometimes the Deciding Factor

High School grades and SAT/ACT scores are other factors that will determine where your son or daughter will be accepted to play. Regardless of how good of a player your son or daughter may be, they may not be accepted to a university because of a grade point average and SAT/ACT requirements. They may be a perfect 4.0 student in high school but if they don't meet the universities minimal qualifications for the SAT/ACT, they are not getting in.

As of the writing of this guide, many schools require a minimum SAT score of 470-550 in Math and 470-550 in English. This is a general range for the universities we have visited. 550 would be for higher academically ranked schools and incrementally lower for smaller state schools. I am sure there are universities that are higher and lower than the ranges above, but this range provides your son or daughter a good target. Check with each university to understand their requirements.

Schools also worry about students with a low GPA in high school and a high SAT score. This shows a lack of discipline and commitment to their studies. I have heard of coaches making offers to kids only later to rescind them since their grades or SAT/ACT scores would not pass the admissions standards. Whatever your son or daughters weakness is in high school, have them work on it now as it may limit their options when the recruiting cycle begins. The good news is there are more and more schools that are admitting students without the SAT/ACT score. Their posture is that a SAT/ACT score is not a good indicator of how a student will perform once at the university. Students are however required to have a high GPA and class ranking in high school.

Students need to stay on top of their studies in high school and steadily improve or maintain their GPAs. In addition, start taking the SAT or ACTs early, perhaps as early as their freshman year in high school. Since you can use the highest score from any of the SAT/ACT test your son or daughter takes, keep taking them until you have achieved the 550 range for both English and Math. Remember, you don't need to communicate test result to the coaches until the visits begin.

Go to the following NCAA site and check out the recruiting and eligibility information (As of 6/2009) *http://www.ncaa.org/wps/ncaa?key=/ncaa/ncaa/legislation+and +governance/eligibility+and+recruiting*

Distance from Home

Another item to consider before beginning the recruiting process is how far away does your son or daughter want to be from home? They may say, and you may agree, the further the better, but distance has an effect on expenses regardless who is saying it! Traveling to games far away may require air travel, hotel, rental cars and possibly taking extra days off from work or attending games becomes unfeasible. Taking your son or daughter to the university at the beginning of every semester and bringing them home can get expensive. Storage of furniture during the summer may also be necessary if the school is not within driving distance. This does not even include Thanksgiving and Spring Break.

Getting Organized and Scheduling Your Visits

When your son or daughter begins to receive letters from coaches expressing interest, be proactive and communicate with them promptly. Setup a recruiting calendar that lists personal days, such as birthdays. Add school activities and club/ODP soccer events to be sure not to double book.
Coaches will want your son or daughter to come for an overnight visit which may include a weekday, such as a Friday/Saturday or a Sunday/Monday. Some coaches do not want their weekends affected and try to schedule visits during the week. If you must do it during the week, I would try to schedule a Monday/ Tuesday, so you can travel on Sunday cutting out a day you would need to be away from work. Make sure you have at least one week day in your schedule since this is a good time for your son or daughter to meet the team and experience going to class with one of the team members.

Do not count out any university at this stage of the process. Be ready to see many schools in a short period of time. Try to piggy-back soccer tournaments with university visits if they are both in the same geographic area. This will help cut some of the travel costs and allow you to see more schools. You do not want to be in the position of having to make a decision with one school when you are just starting the recruiting cycle with another. It is best is to have several schools that are interested in your son or daughter to provide options.

Advance Planning for University Visits

Think about your college visits in advance. This may save you hundreds of dollars over the recruiting cycle. If you need to fly to your destination, allow for at least 2 weeks to book flights. The closer to the flight date the more expensive the tickets. The other suggestion is to rent a car. Using a rental car that is more economical, more comfortable or more reliable than yours and may be cheaper than using your own car and racking up miles.

Ride Sharing

Another cost savings tip for college visits is to ride share. Identify another individual on your soccer team who is being recruited by the same school and coordinate your schedules with the coach. Also, you may find other high school friends, outside of soccer, that are looking at the same school. This will cut your expenditures in half and may make the visit a little more comfortable for the two players or student.

Hotel Arrangements

When making arrangements to visit a college, be sure to ask the coach if the university has certain hotels they deal with for recruiting. Often these hotels offer better rates to families who are visiting the university for recruiting purposes.

Don't Show Off Your Status Symbols

Some coaches, I believe, look at the family and possibly add more money for a needs based athlete. Assuming that this is true, families that show up in a Mercedes Benz compared to a 20 year old Suburban may not get as good an offer. I believe this consideration is made for partial scholarships more than full rides. Just some thing to think about.

Chapter 4

The Coach's Perspective

The bottom line is that coaches need to win. If they fail to win, they are out of a job. Most coaches have contracts that the universities can renew or cancel. So, when it comes to recruiting players they are careful negotiators and want to find the right athletes that can win titles and in turn keep them in a job. To be fair, they also love the game and the competitive nature of college soccer. Coaches that are able to balance their own ambitions with that of the athlete are the more successful coaches. I think really wanting to play for a coach is an overlooked variable in program success.

What Coaches are Looking For in a Player

Coaches are looking for faster, bigger and stronger soccer players, at least that's what I have been told over the last couple of years. Smaller athletes will have a harder time being recruited by the more dominant programs because of their physical limitations. Having weight, height and muscle mass really begins to show in college when play gets tough.

Smaller players have a problem with leverage on and off the ball and the constant pounding will take a toll on their mental and physical health. Coaches are also looking for athletes that have very good technical skills and an excellent understanding of the game with situational experience and knowledge. Where is the player when he or she does not have the ball? For those of you who have sons or daughters who are smaller, they need to make up for their size difference in quickness, speed and soccer brains.

There are other attributes that are important to the coaches. They want kids who are competitive, that don't stop trying until the final whistle, regardless of who is winning or losing. Giving up on a ball at a coach's tournament may be the difference between being recruited and being passed on by a coach. How an athlete fights back when down in the game can be just as important to a coach as scoring an amazing goal.

The entire soccer package is important to coaches. Coaches are interest in "What kind of person am I recruiting?" In one of the coaches' tournaments a coach was standing next to one of our parents watching a game and the subject of my daughter came up. His question was "What kind of a kid is she?" The parent's response was "look at her.. she's always has a smile on her face!" She ended up going to that university.

If your son or daughter is being recruited and is asked to come to the university tour and overnight visit, the coach will ask simple questions to get to know your son or daughter better. Being cocky or non-responsive will not get them far. They also need to realize that they are not only being interviewed by the coach but by the players. Players do have input into the decision process. I have heard of players killing a potential opportunity because of the recruit's social and/or behavioral issues. Have your son or daughter put their best foot forward, smile, relax and be themselves. Finally, warn your son or daughter to stay away from any wild parties during their visit. I have heard of recruits going out with the players and the next day are not able to function because they are hung over.

Finally, coaches want athletes that can stay academically eligible. Having an athlete on their team that can not stay eligible becomes a risk to the team and in some cases creates a void in their roster. In some cases, a coach may choose a slightly less skilled player knowing that the academic eligibility problem will not be an issue.

What Coaches Want and Where to Improve

Players who continually get feedback on their play and work on their weaknesses will show better in Coaches' tournaments. So what are coaches looking for during these events?

Coaches are looking for athletes that are fit and can perform throughout the game. All of us have seen a game won by a team because they were more physically fit than the other. Being able to play at a competitive level from the start to the end of the game is important. Speed is also a multi-dimensional talent that is important to coaches. Can they out accelerate the opposition to create opportunities on the field? How well do they maintain ball control at any speed? Are they able to change direction quickly and change speed to keep the opposition guessing? How strong of a player are they? Are they able to shield the opponent from the ball or run through a physical situation with the ball and maintain possession? Hold players away with upper body strength to create distance to allow a shot? Does the player have good vision on the field and are they able to see opportunities and situations that lead to potential scoring? Do they utilize other players that are close, out wide, across or down field? How creative is the player with pass angles, redirection of play and keeping the other player off balance during possession. Of course there are the other core skills such as dribbling, passing, heading and overall ball control. Being absolutely fluent in all of these areas is a must for a player that wishes to be recruited.

The last skill is being able to finish. Finishing consistently is a rare skill in my observation. Watching a player smell blood and finish with whatever means required is seldom seen and always appreciated by the coach. I am sure I have not mentioned all of the attributes and skills coaches are looking for but this is a good place to start. Additionally, I would ask your club coach and then find out where your son and daughter needs to improve on the field.

Parents... Don't Mess It Up!

Finally... the parent factor! Coaches are very aware that if they recruit the kid they inherit the parents. Whatever you do, do not come to a recruiting visit assuming your child is the best thing since sliced bread. There is **PLENTY** of talent out there and your son/daughter is probably one of several athletes they are recruiting. Do not answer questions directed at your son or daughter, let them speak for themselves. For the long term, be supportive of the coach and other players and finally, stay out of the coach's business. They don't take kindly to parents providing game pointers or questioning your son or daughters playing time. Once your son or daughter is recruited, you are nothing but a team supporting spectator. Being more than a spectator can affect your son or daughters playing time, relationship with the coaches and teammates, or worse yet, their scholarship.

Chapter 5

The Start of the Recruiting Process

It has been my experience that the recruiting process starts as a result of a coach's tournament. Large regional coaches' tournaments will attract several hundred coaches. Players who are on the regional and national teams will surely be recruited based on their merits outside of a coach's tournament, but are also being scouted. The Olympic Development Program "Regional Tournament" occurs once a year and will attract university coaches as well. High school is not the place to get the attention of a coach. They may resort to a high school game only if it is the last chance they have to see an athlete they are really interested in. In all of my years of going to soccer games, I have only seen one college coach at a high school game.

Preparing for Tournaments

Prior to your son or daughters participation in a coaches' tournament, go online and review the list of the universities and coaches that will be attending. Every good tournament has a web page dedicated to the attendees. Review and discuss the list of schools with your son or daughter. Based on your knowledge of the school and their interest, write the name of the schools down on a piece of paper. Using Google or an other search engine, type in the name of the university followed by (Women's) or (Men's) soccer. This will generally guide you to their "official" web site. Look at the roster and select coaches. Write down the Coach and Assistant Coach's names. The next step is to locate their email addresses. On most university web sites there is a tab for Administration / Staff Directory. This is where you can find the coaches email address. If you still can't find their email address, call the athletic department and request it. In addition, fill out the Prospect Questionnaire that is on the soccer web page. You should be able to do this online. Calling the coach is another good option. This should be done after sending them an email and filling out the Prospect Questionnaire.

If your son or daughter knows the area of study they wish to pursue, further work will need to be done. Type in the name of the university in Google or other search engine and look into the curriculum offered at the university to see if it matches their interests. These sites also have some great virtual video tours that may be good to view.

One last note about coaches' tournaments. Make sure that your team will be playing their games at the main location. Clubs who put on the Coaches' tournaments like to grow their "business" and open their tournament to more teams. While this may be good for a club that is on the edge of being considered for the tournament, it can be misleading. In one of the big east coast tournaments, our team was in the tournament but was on fields that were located about twenty-five minutes from the main fields. Parents from these teams had paid hundreds of dollars in travel and lodging costs only to have <u>two</u> coaches stop by and watch. I am sure that if the parents would have known this in advance they would have not made the trip.

Team Profile – A Must

<u>It is extremely important</u> that at each coach's tournament an <u>updated</u> team profile is provided to each coach that is watching. Designate a politically savvy parent to hand out the team profile and keep track of the universities that are watching. This list of universities collected should be distributed to all the parents as soon as possible. Parents should use this list to validate if a coach has followed through on their promise to review your son or daughters play. In some cases, they will continually send information via US Mail or Email, telling you that they will be there and never show up. These are the colleges you don't focus your attention on. Be sure to print enough profiles.. they go fast!

Coaches that do show up will use the profile to identify a player on the field as well as providing them with critical information such as home and email address. Each player should be represented in a tri-fold color presentation of the team. As players commit to schools, the team profile should be updated to reflect this. This will allow others on your team to be looked at for possible consideration.

If players have not met the minimal SAT qualifications mentioned in Chapter 3, I would leave it blank until they can retake the test again. Putting in a low SAT score may scare a coach away. However, if your son or daughter has met or beat the 550 target in Math and English make sure to show it off. This becomes a big plus to a coach as they know the eligibility issue is not a problem. Also, I would not hand out multi-page profiles or individual / personal profiles of a player. Tacky! If you need some ideas for your team's profile, go online and see what some of the other clubs are doing.

Sending Video Tape

In general, soccer coaches have not asked for video tapes and therefore I would not send one. Coaches prefer to see your son or daughter in live action rather than on a tape that may have been edited. The only time to send one is if they ask for it. I have only heard of one coach asking for a video as they were not going to get another chance to watch the player perform before the athlete made their decision.

Sending a Formal Letter of Interest

Once you have the coach's name and email addresses create a form letter for each of the schools your son or daughter is interested in and provide their schedule at the tournament. It should also include the place, time, field and maps if possible. Anything to make it as easy on the coaches as humanly possible. The form letter should be one page and contain the following:

- Introduction paragraph on where you are currently going to school and that you are interested in their university and soccer program
- A paragraph about your current high school successes such as current GPA, Honor Roll, National Honor Society, other academic achievements.
- What club you are currently playing for and what position(s) you play. Also indicate if your club has won any major championships or tournaments recently.
- Insert any other teams you may play on such as ODP, Regional or National Teams and for how long
- Describe your high school soccer career and accolades.
- Provide an upcoming schedule, and if possible location, dates and times. Note: If your schedule changes, which many times it does, be sure to send the coach an update!

Sample letters are also available on the internet.

Prior to July 1st of your son or daughters junior year, the recruiting process almost always begins with a letter or email expressing interest from the Coach or the Assistant Coach. This happens because coaches are not allowed to call athletes directly until July 1st of their junior year in high school. The letter or email can be a form letter or it can be more explicit about seeing your son or daughter play in a specific tournament. Letters that are more specific and personal are of higher interest as they demonstrate an increased level of interest by the coach. The form letter on the other hand, may go out to hundreds of athletes fishing for interest by saying they have seen your son or daughter play at "X" event. I have heard of coaches sending these letters to an entire ODP team making the letter a non-event to the players once the rest of the team finds out. In one situation, the coach accidently sent the letters out saying she saw them play *before* the tournament was actually played. She then followed it up with an embarrassing apology. Always keep your options open and respond to those who have sent letters or email. Ask the coach for more information on the university. Print and keep all correspondence in a paper file and organize it by university. If your son or daughter absolutely knows they are not interested in the inquiring university, be honest and respond to the coach by thanking them for their interest but their university is not one of the universities being considered. A bit of warning, once you've done this, there is no going back most of the time. They will however, appreciate your honesty and move on. <u>An important point in this phase of the process is to build options and leverage for your son or daughter. The best way to do this is by creating interest and nurturing relationships with several schools, not just one.</u>

You Need to Help with the Communication Process

Do not count on your son or daughter to champion the recruiting process. With our eldest daughter, I let her manage email from the coaches and this slowly became a problem. There were many excellent schools emailing her, yet she was not responding to their requests for information and interest. I think this happened as she was not aware enough of the school's programs to make an informed decision. Many key emails were missed, and as a result coaches assumed that there was no interest. With our second, third and fourth daughters, we agreed that they would provide me the password to their email so I could "help them" with the coaches' inquiries. In most cases, they wrote the emails and I reviewed them to ensure I knew who was sending them emails and that their returned responses were written in a positive and accurate manner. If they don't agree with allowing access, try to agree on a secondary email address that both of you share. I also kept track of what the coaches were asking for such as SAT/GPA/High School transcripts and ensured they were returned in a timely manner. Monitor the general information that universities send to your son or daughter. Open this mail with them...be excited for them. In three US mail communications to one of my daughters, they offered her a full scholarship in the cover letter. All she had to do was contact them. Two of the three I didn't even know about until well after the mailing and by then it was too late and the coaches had moved on. Make sure you are a part of the communication process.

Responding to Coaches

As I said above, some universities will send a generic letter to the player's email address to gauge the level of interest before continuing the process. Respond quickly to all letters that are sent. If your son or daughter is highly recruited, you may need to become more selective in your responses, based on volume. Let persistent universities know that you are planning your visits, and ask them to send more information. This will delay the process and allow you to spread the interest out over more time. There is no way to keep more than 7 to 10 university soccer programs in the running at one time and do it well. If need be, keep a list of the universities in a spreadsheet and list the most important attributes your son or daughter is looking for in a school (Coach, Facilities, team members, etc) in each column, rank each area from one to five after your visit (See example on page 48). This may help in the decision process down the line. If your son or daughter is not receiving many recruiting letters they need to handle the ones they do get with kidd gloves. Make sure they respond quickly to their emails and move the process along the best you can. Any athlete not getting many letters from coaches should consider moving through the process faster and making a commitment sooner. You can try and push the coach by calling them. You can call the coach as much as you like as long as you are the one initiating the contact.

University Assessment Score Card

1-Lowest 5 Highest

University	Like Coach(s)	Like University	Facilities	Dorm Room	Tutor /Facility	Like the Girls	Scholarship Offer	Soccer Field	Academics	Total
R University	2	4	3	4	2	3	3	3	4	28
S University	5	2	2	2	2	4	4	2	3	26
T University	1	2	2	1	1	3	5	2	2	19
U University	5	4	4	5	3	4	4	4	4	37
V University	3	3	3	2	2	3	3	3	3	25
W University	3	2	3	2	4	1	2	3	3	23
X University	4	2	4	1	5	2	1	2	3	24
Y University	1	2	1	1	1	2	1	4	3	16
Z University	4	4	3	3	2	2	3	4	4	29

The Campus Visit

At some point in the process the coach will want your son or daughter to come to the school for a visit and possibly stay overnight with the team to get a better feel for the campus. Make sure you get the following information before you visit:

- An Agenda – Many coaches will provide an agenda prior to your visit
- Make sure you have the coach's office and cell phone number in case you have problems
- Don't be late, if you're going to be late for your appointment call and alert the coach
- Confirm where you will meet the coach on campus and get specific directions to that location
- Driver's license (sometimes required to be on campus)
- Money for meals / Lodging (required for unofficial visits)
- Ask for a list of anything else you need to bring with you

As part of the visit, many of the coaches will also want your son or daughter to come to a training session for the team. You, the parent, need to be observant during the campus visit and the training session.

Here is a list of things to observe during your visit:

- When you arrive is the assistant coach there to greet you or is it the coach? How do they react? Do they stand up and greet you and your son a daughter? If the coach believes your son or daughter is something special to his program, he/she will go out of their way to show their interest.
- Does the coach or the assistant coach show your son or daughter around the university? Again, this shows a level of interest.

A Parents' Guide to College Soccer Recruiting

- If at all possible, be at the training session before it starts. Observe the girls/guys coming to practice. Are they happy and smiling? Do they look like they want to be there? How is the interaction between the coaches and the players? How many of the players are hurt/injured? How many are coming to practice with ice bags and sprains? Do all the players seem comfortable with each other? These are all important things to observe. I have made some of these simple observations and in some cases accurately provided valuable insight into team life.
- What is the relationship between the coaches? Do they look like they are having fun or is it a job? (While coaching is a job, it should appear fun to your son or daughter)
- What kind of person is the coach? <u>The number one issue that can ruin a university experience is a coach</u>. A coach can make each day a wonderful, challenging and fulfilling experience, or they can make each day impossible. Trust your instincts.
- Clearly a commitment to the academic success of each player is tied to the programs that a university has established to ensure success in the classroom. Ask if the university has an athlete learning center. This is where student athletes must go to satisfy university study hall requirements. It also has personal computers and tutors. Some schools will have very little in the way of these services and others will have state-of-the-art facilities.
- Check out the athletic facilities. Do they have separate facilities for the athletes and student body? Is the equipment state-of-the-art? Are there specialized fields just for soccer or are there just generic multipurpose fields?

Also prior to the visit, prepare some questions your son or daughter will want to ask the coach. During the tour of the university, the coach will probably ask several times if your son or daughter has questions. Then at the end of the visit, there is a formal sit down with the coach in his/her office. If you have any questions during your tour… write them down. It is very important that your son and daughter be attentive to the coach, have a smile on their face and have fun in the process. Remember, the coach has seen your son or daughter play, they are now looking for what kind of a person they are and how they would fit in with the other players. They want to know if your son or daughter can become a part of their soccer family.

On a visit to a nationally ranked university, one of my daughters took some decongestant right before the meeting with the coach to help with a cold she had. During the discussion with the coach, she was looking around the room and gave off the impression that she was not interest. I was sitting in the meeting, blood boiling, as I couldn't do anything to help the situation. The coach called our club coach the next day and asked if there were any problems with her. Stunned by this, our club coach called me. As soon as I saw his number on my cell phone I said "So she thought she wasn't interested and you're calling to see what went wrong." Our club coach said "yep.. that's pretty much it". In this situation she was given another chance based on our club coach's feedback and the feedback from her ODP coach. But the college coach *did* follow up with these coaches to make sure she was not getting a bad egg should a scholarship be extended. Again, be sure your son or daughter is smiling, attentive and interested in the process!

Here are a couple questions that may provide you some valuable information:

- Where are you (coach) in your recruiting cycle?
- How many athletes are on your roster?

A Parents' Guide to College Soccer Recruiting

- Is your program fully funded? Usually a parent question. <u>Do not ask "How much am I getting!"</u> That will come later, and the coach will tell you.
- Where do you see me playing on your team?
- What is your coaching style and expectations?
- What are the requirements for GPA and SAT scores to be accepted into the university?
- If I get hurt as a result of playing soccer and I am unable to play again, will you honor my scholarship? For how many years? Not all universities will honor their commitment for consecutive years.
- If your son or daughter gets hurt, what kind of medical services will the university provide? How does insurance work?
- What do you expect from me as a player and a student?
- Do the athletes / soccer players room together or within lodging for the student body?
- Can I have a car on campus?
- Will you be the coach when I start at the university? (Contract period)
- How do you schedule soccer practice around my academic schedule?
- Can I get a tutor any time I need it? What's the process for getting one?
- Is there mandatory study hall?
- Are there team building events? If so, what are they?
- If I need to go to summer school, will the university cover my expenses as part of a scholarship?

The next couple of questions are aimed at the players. Your son or daughter can ask some of these questions during their overnight visit or when they are alone with the players.

- What is the coach *really* like?

- Is he/she a yeller? If so when? (In games / practice / all the time)
- What don't you like about him or her?
- What are the assistant coaches like?
- Do the coaches play good cop bad cop and if so who plays what role?
- Is the coach respectful of your personal needs?
- How important is academics to the coach?
- What do you do during pre-season?
- Is college and/or soccer what you expected? Is it different than what you were told?
- What does a typical academic / soccer day look like?
- Would you change your decision if you had a chance?
- What is your favorite/least favorite part of your college soccer experience?
- How much travel is involved? How are missed classes resolved?
- How does the coach motivate you and the team to become better players?
- What's the city / town like?
- Have any players left the team? Why?
- Has the coach ever made you play even though you were hurt?

During their overnight, a specific player(s) on the team is responsible for your son or daughter's visit. This includes a meal at the dining hall, which you will have to pay for unless it is an official visit. One nice thing I tried to do was to provide additional money to my daughter so she could purchase several pizzas or subs for the girls who are responsible for them for the evening. Pizza seemed to get some of the other girls on the team to visit with the hosting players and allow my daughter to get to know the other team members better. They also appreciated the break from the dining hall.

Finally, during your visit, the coach will want to get a read on your son or daughter's interest. Be prepared to answer the following questions: (I have included answers in some of the cases)

- What other universities are you considering? Say "several" and only provide a few of the top schools followed by "and some other Division 1 schools." Some coaches will weigh value based on who is recruiting your son or daughter. Don't make things up as coaches spend time with other coaches and you may get burned. If you have just started the recruiting process, tell them.
- Do you have an area of study you would like to pursue?
- What is your current GPA?
- Have you taken your SAT tests and if so what were your scores?
- What did you think of the university? The answer should be positive.
- Where does it rank compared to the other schools that you are considering? "One of the best" should be the minimum answer.
- What are your strengths and weaknesses on the field?
- Where do you play next? / What tournaments will you be in?
- What did you think of the team members? Be positive
- What is more important, an athletic scholarship or a good school and soccer program?

On the way home from a college visit or the next day, sit down with your son or daughter and write down all the things you have learned. You may need this information later during your decision making process. Also, be sure to have your son or daughter write a thank you note to the coaches and any of the players who helped with their visit.

Lastly, during the final meeting of your visit with the coach, he/she may give you an offer, or they may not. Coaches are not naive and know why you are there. They may say that they need to see you play again before making a decision. Don't be discouraged, this is where the negotiations begin.

Chapter 6

Scholarship Negotiations

Lets be realistic, there is little room for negotiation with a coach unless you have other options. Options are power in the negotiating process. Most coaches have been through this process hundreds of times and know what you're thinking before you even arrive. Most already have an idea of what they can offer and how much money they have to spend. But, there are some things you can do and be aware of in the negotiation process.

Level Set Your Expectations

Unless your son or daughter is on a national team or has exceptional soccer qualities, go into the negotiation process assuming that you will come out with a partial scholarship. Full scholarships really don't happen for the majority of the athletes. Coaches like to spread money around to as many players as possible. As you go through the recruiting process and visit multiple universities, you will begin to see the scholarship value coaches are willing to offer.

Scholarship Discussions

Parents should take an active role in the scholarship negotiation process. After all, anything that is not covered will be your responsibility or will roll to your son or daughter through student loans. They have no idea what kind of liability they are creating for themselves after they graduate. You can possibly help lessen the pain by participating. Usually, when coaches start talking about money they involve the parents.

If you think about recruiting from a commodity perspective it will change your thoughts about how to approach the recruiting process. If you remove your parent/child relationship, athletes can be a valuable asset to a university athletic program. This is especially true in men's sports such as football and basketball. Millions of dollars come into the university as a result of television, other media and marketing rights. It stands to reason that coaches are in competition with other universities for the best players that can help their team. The best position to have your son and daughter in is a position of choice. Ensuring that the coach knows that your son or daughter has choices is important as it increases their scholarship value, but don't be over confident. At some point, they will ask what other programs your son or daughter is considering in the selection process. Be sure to list the best schools first. I would not mention what the offers are at this point in the discussion. If they ask just say "substantial but that is not all that our decision is based on."

In Chapter 5, we discussed the university visit and it is here that coaches make the formal "verbal" offer. The offers can be as simple such as "we will provide a full athletic scholarship" to "we will provide a 75% athletic scholarship." It can get more complex, such as offering an increasing athletic scholarship over four years or combinations such as 50% athletic and 50% academic scholarships, grants etc. Also, coaches may approach the expenses by offering combinations such as paying for tuition but not room, board and books. This is usually where the parent steps in, and in most cases the coach expects it. The following items should be covered by the parent.

- What is the term of the scholarship? In most cases, athletic scholarships are renewed each year. It is a good idea to find out the criteria for the scholarship to be renewed or, more specifically, why they would not be renewed. Some state schools have a four year commitment on scholarships.
- Will the university extend the scholarship to five years to allow an athlete to finish up their degree? Many schools will allow students a 5th year to ensure they keep up their graduating numbers for NCAA purposes. This becomes very important when taking a five year program like engineering.

A Parents' Guide to College Soccer Recruiting

- Ask the coach if they have ever pulled a scholarship and for what reason(s). On one particular university visit, a new coach said that only about 50% of last years team would be continuing next year's season as the others were not up to his standards of play. Wow, what would he do with your son or daughter?
- What is considered part of the scholarship? Tuition, room, board, books, fees, bus transportation etc. Make sure you understand the scope of the offer. You may be surprised in a good way. What is the value of each of the expenses. Be sure to go to the universities' web site before the visit and understand all the costs. This will help you understand what value you are being given.
- If a coach provides your son or daughter a scholarship offer in terms of dollars and not a percentage, be sure to ask him how future university increases in tuition, room, board are absorbed. This will further define your liability.
- If an academic scholarship is extended as part of the package, be sure to understand what GPA must be maintained to continue the scholarship semester-to-semester or year-to-year. What happens if your son or daughter falls short of the GPA target? Will they have another semester to bring their GPA up? Will you, the parent, then have to absorb the academic scholarship if it is pulled? This is a critical decision with an athletic/academic scholarship combination. I am not a big fan of this type of combination. Even the best scholar athletes may have a hard time getting acquainted to the academic demands of the first semester of college.

An Offer is Extended

Once the offer is extended no matter how small, be very appreciative. Be patient. Do not immediately say "yes!" unless you and your son or daughter are absolutely sure this is the right university at the right price. Give your self and your son and daughter some time to think it over and discuss it privately. Never say "no" immediately either. Even if it is a full scholarship, remember the other expenses such as transportation covered in Chapter 2. Also, if there is a full scholarship provided at one school there may be others. Express sincere thanks to the coach and ask them when they need a decision. If the offer is extended by the assistant coach you need to make sure you hear the same information from the head coach. The assistant really has no authority to extend an offer to an athlete. Finally, if a verbal offer is extended, ask the coach to put the offer in an email for "tracking purposes." If your son or daughter wants to accept the offer, respond to the email as such. This will ensure there is no misunderstanding of what was offered and that a formal agreement has been made.

Decision Timeframes

Coaches will generally allow athletes time to visit other schools, however some schools will give your son or daughter a time limit to respond. Where your son or daughter and the coach are in the recruiting process will determine the amount of pressure they will apply for an answer. Some club coach's feel that if they want your son or daughter bad enough they will be willing to wait. I can't say I share that philosophy, there are a lot of great players and coaches know that the recruiting cycle will commit athletes quickly, athletes they may have been interested in.

One thing coaches generally ask for is to stay in communication with them and provide updates on your recruiting process. If a coach stops communicating after your university visit this sometimes means trouble. It is very important for the coach to receive regular communication from your son or daughter and from the coach back to them. If a coach stops communicating with your son or daughter, be persistent. Most coaches will let you know if they are no longer interested. I once asked a coach about how often he wanted to hear from one of my daughters and he said "certainly not every day, but maybe once every 2 weeks." If you are unsure, ask. If your son or daughter has a school that is high on their list of possibilities, and there has been little to no communication from the coach via emails or letters, I think it is appropriate for the parent to send an email asking for an update. If this does not work, call them. At least you and your son or daughter will know and you can move on if necessary.

Write Down What You Liked During Your Visit

Again, once you and your son or daughter return home from a visit, write down the things they liked or didn't like about the school. This will help you remember the university after visiting several others.

Narrowing Down Your Choices

Visit as many other universities as possible and ask the same questions. Narrow down your selection to three schools if possible. If your son or daughter likes a school, the next step is to determine if you can afford the school. In instances where a coach may have given you a percentage of a scholarship, you need to understand what that means. For example, if a school that costs $50,000 a year offers a 50% scholarship, then you are on the hook for $25,000 per year. If you can not afford this cost, I would suggest emailing the coach and ask to talk with him/her. The discussion needs to be an honest one telling them that even with the scholarship being offered, you are unable to afford the school. There are three possible outcomes to this discussion. One, they will tell you that this is all they can offer at this time. Two, they will provide you a better second/third and fourth year percentage. Three they will simply ask what you can afford. If coach responds with the third response, be prepared to give them an honest answer. Expect them to want a verbal commitment should they increase the scholarship. If the answer is sorry, no more money, then no harm done as you were not able to afford it

A Parents' Guide to College Soccer Recruiting

any way. There is always a chance they will increase the offer and you will never know unless you ask.

Keep Your Options Open!

Be sure to keep your university option open and available all the way to the point of the verbal commitment. This will give you a fall back plan should something happen in the recruiting process with another school.

Greed will Turn on You

While in the negotiation process, don't get greedy or demanding. This will surely backfire. It is important to remember that full scholarships are not that common. Knowing this will help guide you to a reasonable offer.

I heard a story where a coach made a full offer to a young lady but books were not included. The father tried to take it further to include books. The coach denied the plea and the parent continued to pressure the coach to include books by making it a contingency to accepting the offer. The coach called the club coach and asked about the parent. The club coach was so aggravated at the parent that they refused to help with other recruiting queries. In the end, the college coach passed on the opportunity. The young lady had no other full ride scholarships to fall back on and her dad ended up having to pay 50% of a bill at another school.

Sometimes They Come Back

If a coach does not make an acceptable offer, or any offer at all, leave the conversation in a positive and professional manner. Have your son or daughter express to the coach what they liked about the university, his/her team and him or her as a coach. They really appreciate sincere people and in some cases they will

A Parents' Guide to College Soccer Recruiting

revisit the offer should they get the opportunity. Leaving it poorly will only reinforce their decision.

Reconfirm Your Choices If Necessary

Getting your selection down to two or three universities will allow you to focus on these schools even more. If you have to, visit the university with your son or daughter again. Walk around the college without the coach. Visit the town that the college is in and see what it has to offer. After all, you will be spending many weekends there watching the games. If you have a chance, go to one of their home games and sit with the parents. Parents will give you a pretty fair assessment of everything from the team, to the coach, to the university. Be careful to talk with more than one parent as their always seems to be one disgruntled parent on every team. Also, check out the roster and see what cities the players are from. Try to find someone from your area that you can talk to by phone. Find out where the coach was before coaching at the university. It is amazing what you can learn by doing a little research. It IS a small world!

If You Can't See It, It's Not There

Finally, remember that if a coach really wants a player, they will go to any length to seal the deal. In my visits, I have heard stories from universities stating that the board of directors has developed a capital plan to rebuild part of the campus and athletic facilities and most of the construction should be completed by their freshman year. Needless to say, it didn't happen and thank goodness we didn't hang our hat on it. Only focus on what the university has to offer today. Tomorrow may never come.

University Acceptance – Important

As part of the recruiting process, the coach must also determine if the athlete meets the university academic requirements. As stated

A Parents' Guide to College Soccer Recruiting

in Chapter 3, each university requires a minimal SAT/ACT score and GPA. Make sure you ask the coach if your son or daughter meets these requirements. In some cases, coaches will ask the admissions office to perform an "initial read" of your son or daughter's transcripts and SAT/ACT scores. If your son or daughter does not meet the requirements, the coach may give him/her more time to improve their scores. You need to hear the words "Yes – he/she meets the schools academic requirements" and, if possible, get it in writing. You do not want to be engaged later in the formal admission process only to find out you do not meet the SAT/ACT requirements and have no other recruiting options.

Twins and the Negotiation Process

When coaches see twins on a team they will assume in most cases that they are a "Package Deal." They may be looking for a forward but see a twin and assume they must take both players. I think a key point in the positioning of twins is to truthfully understand their skill level, independent of each other. I would get this assessment from your coach so you will understand what a college may be willing to invest in them. Going into the discussion with a university coach, I think it is important that the coach understand they are *not* a package deal. The only time not to do this is if the twins absolutely want to go to school together. The discussion about going to school with or without each other should happen long before the recruiting process begins. When university coaches deal with twins, they generally tend to be fair, but will provide a split in scholarship or in some cases offer one more than the other. This may not mean that the other twin is less valuable, it just means they are not what the coach needs to complete his team. By telling a college coach that your twins are not a package deal during your visit to the university, you are telling them that they intend to go to school where they individually prefer and in the process should open the door, possibly, for more money. If you have one twin that has

A Parents' Guide to College Soccer Recruiting

excellent soccer skills yet the other does not, settling for a package deal may be in your best interest.

Chapter 7

Making the Decision

The last step in the recruiting process, the decision, can be the
hardest for your son or daughter. In some cases they have
created multiple relationships with the coaches and his/her
assistants and players. Other times it is a simple decision.
Hopefully the decision will not be based solely on money but
what is the best university, coach and environment for your son
or daughter. After all, going to college should be one of the best
experiences of their life.

Things to Think About

One of the first things to think about when making the final
decision is "Where am I in the soccer recruiting cycle?" As
stated in Chapter 2, the recruiting cycle begins and ends at
different times based on the school and the Division. High end
Division 1 schools complete their recruiting some where between
December and February of the athlete's Junior year. This may
occur a lot earlier at some big name universities. Small Division
1/ 2 and Division 3 schools may end their recruiting in the
athlete's senior year. During the recruiting process, money
begins to dry up as athletes commit verbally.

Knowing the cycle will give you some idea of where you are in
the process and if there is money available. I have personally
experienced this by not being aware of the recruiting timeline of
a specific school. By the time my daughter contacted the school
and they observed her play, they had already exhausted their
funds for her freshman class.

At Some Point, The Decision Will Be Made

Coaches for the most part are pretty patient, however, at some
point they will need a decision. They don't want to get caught
with a player saying no and possibly losing another player in the
process. It's a timing game and coaches deploy many tactics to

delay or push a decision. The key is to not to keep a coach waiting too long.

One technique mentioned in Chapter 6 is a more direct one. Ask the coach when they would like the decision. If you are not comfortable with the date, you can ask for more time. If they can't wait you may want to speed up your visits. A coach may also ask for a decision as they are afraid they may lose the athlete to another school. Getting an offer from one school may put you in the favorable position of pressuring another coach into a decision/offer. It seems that everyone wants what other people have.

If The University is Great But the Scholarship Isn't

If you do not receive a full scholarship from the university of your choice, a good suggestion is to ask the coach if they can reevaluate your son or daughter for more money in future years. If they say yes, it provides your son or daughter a platform to come back to the coach and ask for more money in the future. This becomes especially relevant if your son or daughter does well in their first year of college soccer. I would suggest asking this question via email so you have the answer in writing. Be sure to specify a time when you will ask again. The best time to ask is in the fall at their end of the season meeting with the coach.

On the other hand, coaches may surprise you by providing other financial assistance. With one of my daughters, she received a partial athletic scholarship which she accepted. Seven months after the initial offer, the school provided a significant academic scholarship that greatly reduced our financial burden. This was all done without a word from the coach. The notice of academic scholarship came with her official acceptance to the university and was a wonderful surprise.

The University Versus the Coach

I hope none of my readers will need to go through the brain shredding process of "I love the university but I don't like the coach." As stated earlier in this guide, the coach can make or break your university experience. If your son or daughter does not like the coach and you have been able to verify with other athletes and parents that there is a problem, my advice is don't go there. One soccer player told me that a coach had made her experience so miserable that if it wasn't for the financial implications to her family, she would have quit after her freshman year.

The Verbal Commitment

When you are ready to make a decision, the coach and your son or daughter will make a verbal commitment to each other. This means you will end your recruiting process with other universities and the coach will stop recruiting for that spot on the team. This is like a hand shake in the old days, when a hand shake really meant something. Do athletes break their verbal commitments? Unfortunately, yes they do. It is not until February of the athlete's senior year that they sign the "Letter of Intent." This is more like a contract between you, the athlete and the university. If, in the end, your son or daughter is not happy with the university once they are there, they can transfer to another school and get out of the agreement with the university. There are usually stipulations attached, so be careful if this route is taken. In addition, after a verbal commitment is given, some coaches may ask for something from your son or daughter as part of the agreement. One request may be to show up for training camp in tip-top physical condition and/or to review their training and play book before coming to summer training camp. Others may request that you forgo high school soccer to ensure you don't get hurt before your first year.

The Official Visit After the Verbal Commitment

After your son or daughter has made a verbal commitment, usually in their senior year of high school, the coach will most likely invite them to the university for an "Official Visit." Normally, the coach will try to get all of the recruits to the university for their Official Visit on the same weekend during their soccer season. This visit is very important for your son or daughter. Sometimes, coaches will pair up freshmen players to room together. It will provide them a chance to meet the other recruits in a social situation and possibly meet a compatible person/roommate. If your son or daughter has the opportunity to meet and hopefully select a roommate during the official visit weekend, it may work to their advantage rather than having the coach do it. Roommates that don't get along can make for a long semester. If your son or daughter finds someone they get along with, make sure that both parties tell the coach of their desire to room together. Following up with the coach again on your selection prior to summer training camp would also be a good idea.

Behavior That Negatively Effects Verbal Commitments

Once the verbal commitment has happened, your son or daughter is still on the hook to keep the agreement intact. Many universities will require the student to maintain a certain GPA and possibly take advance placement classes in their senior year of school. The university will also follow up with a request for transcripts to ensure your son or daughter still qualifies to get into the school.

The other area a school will watch is behavior. If your son or daughter becomes involved in something illegal or is expelled from their high school, universities have been know to revoke the verbal commitment and scholarship offer.

A Parents' Guide to College Soccer Recruiting

Last Order of Business in the Process

Each student athlete who wants to participate in NCAA athletics must register with the NCAA Clearinghouse. The NCAA Clearinghouse evaluates each player to ensure they are academically eligible. Work with your guidance counselor / advisor to register. The registration fee is usually around $60.

Suggestions Once They Start

One of the hardest skills that your son or daughter will need to master is time management. Their spare time will be limited and being able to fit school, practice and fun into their schedule will be very important, especially in their first year of school. To my knowledge, all schools offer time management classes at the beginning of each semester. I would strongly suggest doing this based on their hectic schedule and time away from school when on the road. Most universities provide free formal tutoring for athletes. Make sure your son or daughter take immediate advantage of the tutoring programs in any of the difficult classes they're taking. Waiting to request tutoring until there is a problem may be too late.

Extended Family

Once your son or daughter is off to school they will have a great support structure. One thing my girls have all talked about is the family away from home. Simply being on a soccer team introduces them to a group of kids who all look out for each other. They go to breakfast, lunch and dinner together and have been known to poke a little fun at the coach by calling him dad or mom in public places. Most teams grow as a group and develop a closeness that is not experienced by the average student. When the average student comes to a school they sometimes just know one person, their roommate. Your son and daughter will have an instant family once a way, so relax. These are memories that they will never forget.

I hope for the best for your son or daughter. All of my girls have really enjoyed their experience while being a student-athlete. What a great time of their lives!

Made in the USA
Lexington, KY
23 November 2013